Graduate Your Homeschooler in Style

Make Homeschool Graduation Memorable

Lee Binz,

The HomeScholar

First Printing, 2015

Printed in the United States of America

Cover Design by Robin Montoya
Edited by Kimberly Charron

ISBN: 1511514353
ISBN-13: 978-1511514354

Disclaimer: Parents assume full responsibility for the education of their children in accordance with state law. College requirements vary, so make sure to check with the colleges about specific requirements for homeschoolers. We offer no guarantees, written or implied, that the use of our products and services will result in college admissions or scholarship awards.

Graduate Your Homeschooler in Style

Make Homeschool Graduation Memorable

What are Coffee Break Books?

Graduate Your Homeschooler in Style is part of The HomeScholar's Coffee Break Book series.

Designed especially for parents who don't want to spend hours and hours reading a 400-page book on homeschooling high school, each book combines Lee's practical and friendly approach with detailed, but easy-to-digest information, perfect to read over a cup of coffee at your favorite coffee shop!

Never overwhelming, always accessible and manageable, each book in the series will give parents the tools they need to tackle the tasks of homeschooling high school, one warm sip at a time.

Everything about these Coffee Break Books is designed to suggest simplicity, ease and comfort—from the size (fits in a purse), to the font and paragraph length (easy on the eyes), to the price (the same as a Starbucks Venti Triple Caramel Macchiato). Unlike a fancy coffee drink, however, these books are guilt-free pleasures you will want to enjoy again and again!

Table of Contents

Introduction

Prepare to Launch!

Graduation from high school is a big deal. Most people want to celebrate, share their success with others, and take lots of pictures. If you intend to graduate your child from high school, you need to make a plan for graduation, because there are a lot of details to take care of!

Begin planning for graduation early in senior year. February is not too early to begin planning! If your child is an excellent singer or public speaker and wants to be involved in a larger group graduation ceremony, applications for these positions usually close early in the spring. The last few months of high school go by in a whirl, so prepare early for the final celebration, so you too can celebrate your accomplishments!

The road to graduation takes planning and forethought, not only for the culminating celebration, but also to make sure your child has learned and accomplished everything you want them to before you launch them. In addition to the celebratory aspects of graduation, you'll also find some guidelines to make your child's senior year (and beyond) a successful and joyful experience.

Congratulations and good luck!

Chapter 1

The Graduation Ceremony

For many families, the point of a graduation ceremony is to recognize the graduate. The first step is often to get graduation portraits. We had two sets of senior portraits taken—casual digital photography and formal senior portraits taken by a professional photographer. If you take 200 pictures of your child, surely one of them will be good enough to call a senior portrait!

Announcements are important if you want to let your friends and relatives in on the occasion. I recommend buying announcements early, because it can take a while for them to be printed and shipped to your home. For help with these, I recommend checking out www.homeschooldiploma.com. They are the best company to deal with and have everything you need. When I was ready to graduate my children, I relied heavily on their expertise. Remember to include the graduation photo with your announcement, as people love grad pictures.

As you spend time organizing the graduation ceremony, consider the many options available; for instance, you can celebrate at home or participate in recognition at your church. Many churches give teenagers the option to wear their cap and gown at a recognition ceremony.

Local homeschool groups or state homeschool groups often offer graduation ceremonies, and there are also national events. One of the national events is at Disneyland! Plan ahead if you want to participate in one, as they often fill quickly. You can participate in a group graduation, and then have an individual ceremony or reception at your own home. Ask your teenager what they would prefer. Unless you ask your child, you may not know what they want. I know some homeschoolers that didn't want to have any sort of recognition ceremony for graduation. Instead, parents and child went to a special dinner or lunch. Your child's graduation celebration should be whatever fits your family.

As you plan the graduation ceremony, consider a few things to make it a bit more fun. Playing "Pomp and Circumstance," the song that's normally played during graduation, adds to the festive environment. You can easily download it online.

Some people say a few words: a blessing, dedication, praise, list of accomplishments, Scripture. I gave the task of choosing to my husband, because

I knew that I would be so busy with the food, the party, and the emotions that I wouldn't be able to speak well. One tip is to write down what you want to say, because this is an emotional time—more emotional for parents than for the child! This is such a meaningful time, the end of one phase and the beginning of another for parents. At some point in the ceremony, make sure to present your student with their diploma and shake their hand to make it official. You want them to remember they *did* receive a high school diploma!

Graduation Traditions

One of the most significant graduation traditions is to get a diploma and a diploma cover. As mentioned, HomeschoolDiploma.com is a great place to find these and all your other graduation needs. There may come a time in the future when your children are asked whether they have a high school diploma. You want them to say

"Yes" without hesitation because they remember the big tradition of you awarding them with their diploma.

Many students also wear a cap (complete with tassel) and gown. You can also include "bling" in the ceremony if you want! Purchase honor medallions, honor cords, or class rings. When our son attended college graduation, he received a variety of things for the different majors he completed.

A cap and gown are generally reusable, so you can use them for other children as they graduate. If your child graduates with a group, sometimes the group will require a certain color of cap and gown. The tassel for the cap is often considered a keepsake. Some people put it on the rearview mirror of their car or save it in a chest.

There are a million right ways to hold a graduation ceremony. It can be casual or elegant, depending on your budget, your wishes, and your child's wishes. Ultimately, it should reflect your family and your student.

Double Graduation

For twins and siblings who share a graduation in the same year, there are a couple of unique things to consider. First, don't assume that both students have share the same ceremony. You can choose to have their graduation on the same day or on separate days. My sons are two years apart, but they graduated at the same time, so we decided to hold their graduation on the same day. My son has since married a woman who is a twin, and they went to public school and graduated on the same day, too. You can decide what works best for your family.

Decide whether your kids will share the same cake, guests, and celebration. You could choose a completely different party for each child, and invite the same friends or different friends. We chose to send an individual announcement for each child even though they were sent to many of the same people, because I wanted each of their graduations to be special. And I wanted the opportunity for people to recognize that both of my boys were graduating at the same time. Of course, I also gave them each an individual diploma, but we did combine the party.

We made it a little different, though, by giving them each their own color: red for one and blue for the other. We decorated the table with red napkins and blue napkins. If you're trying to save money, I highly recommend the red and blue, because you can get a lot of inexpensive partyware when you shop after the 4th of July!

Chapter 2

Memories and Mementos

At almost every graduation ceremony I've been to, memories or mementos are displayed that celebrate the graduate. Everyone learns more about the graduate by seeing some of their history.

I prepared photo albums for each of my children. I reproduced some of the best photos from their childhood, and put them into a photo album. We gave one to each of them as a graduation gift, to have when they moved to their own home.

Many parents put together digital slideshows and run a slideshow during the party or graduation. You can also make a professional video slideshow. We used Animoto, which I recommend. These photos became an activity for the adults during the graduation party. Once the kids arrived, they all went to the backyard and played, but the adults hung out around and spent most of their time enjoying the slideshow.

Memory boards have become a popular way to share a graduate's life. In fact, many of the organizations that hold large group ceremonies ask their graduates to bring a memory board. Memory boards are easy to put together. Just choose photos, certificates, newspaper articles, or anything that's significant to your child. Then purchase a foam board from an office supply store and start gluing everything on. You can also print words out and to paste around the pictures.

I also encourage students to share their homeschool transcript and records with others at the graduation. This will help other parents who are homeschooling high school. If they see you did it successfully, they might believe that they can do so as well. Other homeschoolers will benefit from your expertise.

I also recommend that you have a table displaying special activities or interests your child has, such as chess. I included a poem my son had published in a book, which I printed out, because it was a significant memory for him. At other graduations I've attended, the graduates placed their certificates and trophies on a table for everybody to look at.

I have a friend whose daughters made a scrapbook for guests to look through to see their memories. She also had senior portraits framed with a big, white mat. Their guests signed the mat that framed the pictures, as a memento to remind them who came to their graduation.

In a public or private school, students might get a yearbook, and you can make a yearbook for your homeschool. Some people might call it a scrapbook, but you can call it a yearbook.

You could have a guestbook or a framed photo for people to sign at the door. We used a book by Dr. Seuss called *Oh, the Places You'll Go!* It's quite a large book, with a lot of room on each page. I provided a pen and guests signed any page in the book. It was fun, and each of my children has one of these books as a memento from their party.

Save your memories. The time goes by quickly, and the day of graduation goes by even more quickly. Enjoy the moment, take a deep breath, and relax from time to time. Make sure to take lots of pictures!

Chapter 3

Party Ideas

When our sons graduated, we held games outside for the teenagers. We knew it was important to have something for both young and old to do, as many people who came to our homeschool party were older. The young kids only wanted to go play, but the adults seemed to enjoy looking over information about our homeschool.

It was a good opportunity for me to educate both homeschoolers and non-homeschoolers about what homeschooling was like for us. However, the ideas for party themes and ideas are as unique as the families who celebrate!

You can decorate any way you want. You'll find many specific graduation decorations at a party store. Some of the decorations will indicate a specific year, but others will simply say "Congratulations," so if you go to a party store after the graduation season (in July), you can buy discounted items in the graduation color you want and use them the following year. You could also pick a theme, such as Mexican or a luau and decorate as part of that theme. Choose your colors or theme early on so you have enough time to get everything together.

One great graduation idea is to have a Hope Chest Party. You can invite the guests to bring a present to contribute to the hope chest of the girl who's graduating. If a boy is graduating, you can have a Tool Chest Party, where the guests bring a tool for the work chest. Invite people who are unable to attend the party to send a videotaped message and include that message as part of your slideshow.

You can throw an open-house party with simple sandwiches, or a formal party with tablecloths and fresh flowers. Consider a dessert buffet—chocolate fountains are popular among the wedding crowd, and would be fun for a graduation party as well! A simple ice cream sundae bar might be great for your crowd. When I was in college, we got a gigantic plastic (clean) gutter, and filled the whole thing with scoops of ice cream and all the toppings. If you're a scrapbooker, you could put out scrapbooks and supplies for people to create pages for your child.

Some parents rent a hall or a church for their reception and graduation ceremony. You might choose to have either a lunch or buffet, picnic style or formal. Like each wedding celebration is unique, your child's graduation can be unique as well.

Some homeschoolers arrange a prom for their own graduate and their friends. And have dance lessons as part of the graduation party. Some have a guest speaker or their pastor speak at graduation.

If you are planning a party, it's best to avoid holding it the same day as any local public school graduations, because some of your friends may not be able to attend.

Thank You Notes

Sending thank you notes is an important (and almost lost) art, but hopefully you have taught your children to write thank yous. One method to make sure they get written is to hold the gifts hostage until the note is done, or to make sure your teenager writes them before they cash the checks or use the gift cards.

You can find graduation thank you note cards at HomeschoolDiploma.com to coordinate with your graduation announcements. Graduation announcements at an office supply or craft store will often have coordinating thank you notes as well.

Chapter 4

Senior Year Essentials

Senior year is a busy time in a homeschooler's life, for both parent and student. There's so much to do! For those who are planning to go, senior year is all about applying for college. There are many steps in this process, so preparation is key. For the best results, you want to hit the ground running during this last year of high school.

Starting to fill out college applications on the first day of senior year isn't too early. In fact, if your student plans on dual enrollment during their senior year, starting applications before school starts will help. College applications can be complicated; they involve technically perfect, self-reflective essays, which can be difficult to write and take time. Make sure you put plenty of time aside.

Applications also include some complex forms, with many questions, and you need to compile letters of recommendation as well. To get recommendation letters, you must brainstorm on who to ask with your child, and then your child needs to ask them. For some reason, it takes kids quite a bit of time to work up the nerve to ask somebody to write them a letter of recommendation. After they ask, you should allow a lot of time for that person to write the recommendation. Once they write it, allow some time for them to mail it directly to the college. As you can see, a letter of recommendation is not something that can happen overnight; it takes plenty of planning ahead.

Applying for college is remarkably like filling out your federal tax forms for April 15th. There are firm deadlines with strange expectations, a whole bunch of fine print, words you don't understand, and if you mess up, there's a huge financial consequence in the end. Plan ahead and spend time on it, making sure you start by the first day of senior year.

Another important task during senior year is to fill any gaps in your child's education. You can repeat tests if your student needs to improve SAT or ACT scores. If you find any major educational gaps, you can make sure to cover them during senior year. If, for example, your child hasn't started to study a foreign language required by the college that your student wants to attend, they could take foreign language at a community college. One year of foreign language at community college is equal to two or three years of high school foreign language, so community college can be a way to quickly fill a gap. Take this opportunity to make sure your senior has all the requirements he needs before graduation.

For more about what needs to be completed during senior year, see my book, *Senior Year Step-by-Step* on my Amazon author page:

amazon.com/author/leebinz

Chapter 5

College Packing List

It is an exciting day for some and sad for others—the day your graduate moves out of your home to college! Before they head out on this new adventure though, they need to pack! When you consider how small the typical dorm room is, this clearly becomes a challenging process. On one hand, they need to avoid borrowing everything from their neighbors, but they also don't want to arrive with a pod full of stuff that won't fit in a tiny dorm room. Space is usually at a premium, so think of efficiency as you plan.

The following is a list of things that will likely be needed during the year. Some things may be restricted by your child's university, so check their policies before buying electrical equipment, such as microwaves, refrigerators, and toaster ovens.

If possible, try to have your child contact their future roommate(s) prior to arrival. They can coordinate supplies so you don't have two of everything cluttering up the space. If one roommate buys the microwave and the other gets the refrigerator, you both save money. And young women particularly seem to like to coordinate their decorations.

There is probably no end to the list of items a college student might want to pack. With this list, they should have what they need most—except for you, of course. They will still need you and need to know you love them, so keep in touch!

Bedding and Décor

- Dorm Bedding Set (Tip: Get reversible quilts, because they get dirty. Dorm sets like these are often cheaper. Remember, these don't have to be high quality, they only need to last 4 years.)

- 2 sets of bath towels, hand towels, washcloths

- 1 or 2 sets of extra-long twin sheets and pillowcases

- Twin size extra-long mattress pad

- Blankets

- Pillow

- Bedspread or comforter

- Cozy throw blanket (both of my children loved this one!)

- Closet shoe organizer or under-bed storage box

- Over-the-door coat rack

- Posters, photos, artwork

- Calendar

- Message board for door if not provided

- Dry-erase markers

- Magnets for message board

- Small area rug

- Floor pillow or beanbag chair

- Lamps or clip-on lights

- Pictures of family, friends and/or pets

- Decorative shower curtain if needed

- Anything to decorate the room and make your child feel at home

Technology

- Laptop Computer (Tip: Even techie teens may not know how to maintain and care for technology, so service protection is a good investment.)

- Printer with ink

- Surge protector

- Three prong extension cords

- Ethernet cord and/or wireless router

- Television (optional in this day and age of streaming on the computer)

- DVD/Blu-Ray player for the TV plus DVDs to watch (optional)

- Netflix/Hulu Plus/Amazon membership

- Stereo, radio, iPod, headphones

- Compact speaker system

- Flash drive for portable file storage

- Digital camera (optional if they prefer using their smartphone)

- Rechargeable batteries with charger

- Cell phone (and charger) with good service/coverage at the college

School Supplies

- Textbooks

- Pens

- Pencils, mechanical pencils

- Notebooks

- Binders

- Folders

- Highlighters

- Dry-erase markers

- Markers

- Scissors

- Stapler

- Printer paper

- Calculator

- Desk storage tools

- Planner/calendar

- Rubber bands

- Paper clips

- Thumb tacks, push pins, or Sticky Tac to put up posters

- Sticky notes

Kitchen Supplies

- Small Refrigerator, or a micro-fridge combo unit (Tip: As with all electronics, make sure you check the university policy first as they may severely restrict the size of the refrigerator you can bring, if any!)

- Microwave
- Coffee maker/espresso machine
- Can opener
- Toaster/toaster oven (if allowed)
- Hot pad (if allowed)
- Microwaveable plates
- Microwaveable cups or mugs
- Microwaveable Bowls
- Glasses/cups
- Forks, knives, spoons
- Cutting knife
- Cleaning supplies
- Hand soap
- Dish soap

- Disinfectant wipes

- Nonabrasive bathroom cleanser

- Dusting spray/cloths

- Sponges

Clothing

- Mark all clothing with a Sharpie!

- Bathrobe

- Slippers

- Shower shoes, flip flops, or Crocs

- Underwear (1 month's supply)

- Raincoat

- Light jacket

- Winter/heavy coat

- Mittens, scarf, hat

- Rain shoes/boots

- Swimsuit(s)

- Workout and/or sports clothes

- "Dress" clothes and shoes (guys, this means a blazer, tie, or suit)

- "Grubby" clothes

- Comfortable clothes and shoes you can go to class in

Toiletries

- Bathroom tote or toiletry bag (to carry and hold toiletries)

- Toothbrush, toothpaste, dental floss

- Brush and comb

- Shaving equipment

- Hair dryer/straightener/curling iron

- Shampoo

- Conditioner

- Bath soap

- Cotton swabs

- Kleenex/tissues

- Ear plugs

- Bandages/first aid supplies

- Headache, cold, flu, and allergy medicine

Laundry

- Tote-able Laundry basket or bag

- Laundry soap

- Iron, small ironing board

- Hangers

- Quarters for laundry

- Stain remover

- Knowledge of how to do laundry or money to pay someone else to do it

Food

- Vitamins

- Snacks to supplement campus food

- Coffee, tea, soda, bottled water

Miscellaneous

- Alarm clock (Tip: Practice using the new alarm clock before they leave, so they get used to it. Plug-ins are hard to find, so get a good battery-operated alarm clock.)

- Backpack

- Battery-powered flashlight

- Sports/recreation equipment

- Umbrella

- Air freshener and Febreze

- Duct Tape

- Bottle opener

- Storage crates

- Full-length mirror

- Multi tool or hammer, screwdriver, pliers

- Sewing kit

- Electric fans

- Bike and bike lock

- Sleeping bag (for retreats)

- Small bookshelf

- Decorative storage boxes

Documents

- Driver's license or state ID

- Health insurance card

- Social security card

- Health records

- Friends and family contact list

- Access to money (e.g. bank account, bank card, credit card, etc.)

What to Leave Home

Don't have your child bring things they do not or will not use. Don't bring anything expensive they won't use (such as letterman jackets, for example). They should leave behind firearms, even if your child hunts or shoot for sport. Leave behind expensive clothes and jewelry that may be stolen. And sorry, they can't bring their pets. I do know plenty of college kids that bring a stuffed animal, though, and a cozy blanket can be comforting during moments of homesickness or sickness.

Chapter 6

From Homeschool to College: What Scripture Has to Say

When parents and teens begin to transition between homeschool and college, a change of mindset is required. It is okay for our children to grow up. While they were children, we kept them at home, but at a certain point, they're not children anymore. It's okay to allow them to leave as adults.

There are several scriptures which have been helpful to me as our family made this transition from children at home to children at college. I hope they will be encouraging to you as well. The first one is 1 Corinthians 13:11:

> When I was a child, I spoke like a child, I thought like a child, I reasoned like a child. But when I became a man, I gave up childish ways.

This scripture helps us understand that it's okay to shelter your children when they're younger, and it is also okay for them to put away being a child and become an adult, ready to make decisions.

The next scripture is from Mark 16:15, where Jesus tells his disciples to "go into all the world and preach the gospel to all creation." It's common for people to use this scripture against homeschooling, but it's important to note that these words were spoken to adults. While this scripture doesn't apply to children, it does apply to our children once they're grown. Then it's time for them to go into all the world and preach the gospel to all creation.

The last verse I'd like to share comes from Proverbs 22:6: "Train up a child in the way he should go—and when he is old, he will not depart from it." This verse demonstrates three stages of parenting. The first stage is training up your child, which is your job when your child is little. The dash in the middle of the verse is the second stage, and is when the child is responsible to act on how they have been trained. The third stage is "when he is old," the time of God's promise of the result. Of course, the term "when he is old" does not come with a date, so you don't know when it will be! But it is a promise that parents should hold onto.

Remember, your child will grow up eventually, and you must recognize that they have achieved adulthood. It then becomes your prayer that they will remember Exodus 20:12: "Honor your father and your mother, so that you may live long in the land the Lord your God is giving you."

Chapter 7

Letting Go When Homeschooling Ends

Homeschoolers seem to have one thing in common—they love their children. They love having children, they love being around their children, and they love having their children live at home. When the end of homeschooling comes around, the biggest questions parents have is, "When did my baby grow up?" Of course, homeschool children are not always perfectly behaved, and life is not always blissful. I've been a homeschool parent, so I know this isn't true! We're all a little sad when it comes time to let the kids go. But like baby birds that fly the nest, when it's time, it's time.

If college and career is in your student's future, check out my College Launch Solution here. Learn everything you need to become your child's best college coach, and save thousands over hiring a private coach.

Letting go is a season of life not without challenges. I can help you to understand the process, so you are prepared for what lies ahead. While homeschooling, you can ready your child for independent living and make plans for your empty nest. However, you also need to understand what happens when your child is almost an adult but still learning the ropes of independence. You see, the consequences of ignoring the inevitable can cause "Failure to Launch," also called "The Couch Potato Phenomenon." Once your child is grown, you need to learn to set boundaries, so they can thrive and become independent—like you and I became independent from our parents.

Homeschooling can be a huge advantage to launch your teen successfully in this upcoming stage of life.

Prepare to Launch: Understand the Seasons of Parenting

When you take your child to college, it's only one step on the path to independence. Other steps follow.

• The first summer they live away from home.

• The first post-college apartment.

• The first holiday away from home.

Saying goodbye at college is as important as the other goodbyes. Each step has its own emotions, ranging from tears to relief.

Homeschool parents assume four primary roles throughout their children's lives: caretaker, teacher, mentor, and friend. The last season of homeschooling - which promises to last the longest—is the season of friendship. Finally, you and your kids are equals. You may find yourself learning as much (or more) from them as they do from you.

When the kids are grown and gone, take a deep breath and relax. You have a wonderful, life-long friendship to look forward to. The key to enjoying this friendship is up to you. You need to stop homeschooling this child. Provide guidance and counsel when asked, but hold back on unsolicited advice. Enjoy their friendship. You deserve it.

Training Teens: Prepare for Independent Living

Someday your child will live on their own. They will sink or swim based on the skills you have given them, their adult choices, and their ability to adapt as an adult. This basic checklist of independent living skills will help you identify what may need work. They will leave home with these skills or without them, so try to cover them throughout the four years of high school, so they can survive and thrive!

The ability to combine academics with character education, and bring truly well-rounded and grounded young people into the world is one of the joys of homeschooling. To do this, you need to be conscientiously preparing your teen to live independently. They need life skills, such as cooking and cleaning, training and information on finances, employment, and safety. Your child needs to understand how to function socially in groups, while being safe in their mode of transportation. They need to be able to monitor their own education, become successful in college, and graduate with a great GPA so they get a good job.

None of this happens without some training. Like all the other subjects you teach your child, these independent living skills must be taught or discussed first, so the teen understands the concepts and what is expected. Each skill should be demonstrated by the parent or another mentor before it is practiced by the teen. It can take quite a bit of practice before independent living skills are perfected.

This basic checklist of independent living skills will help you identify what may still need work. They will leave home with or without these skills, so try to cover them over the four years of high school so they can survive and thrive!

Live Independently

- Make breakfast, lunch, and dinner
- Wake up on time
- Do laundry Iron clothes
- Make the bed
- Clean a bathroom
- Clean a house
- Unclog a toilet

- Kill unwanted bugs
- Pack a suitcase
- Go grocery shopping
- Change a smoke detector battery
- Take care of belongings
- Identify spiritual beliefs

Social skills

- Order at a restaurant
- Calculate a tip
- Plan a date or outing
- Be sexually responsible
- Be assertive
- Help others
- Advocate for those who can't help themselves
- Maintain healthy relationships
- Vote

Transportation

- Pump gas
- Take public transportation
- Change a tire

- Call a taxi, shuttle, or other transportation
- Talk to strangers
- Drive safely
- Water safety
- Use a map

Finances

- Pay bills
- Create budget
- Balance a checkbook
- Live on a fixed budget
- Track spending
- Pay Taxes

Education

- Monitor school grades
- Keep track of assignments
- Register for classes
- Navigate to classes
- Take notes
- Write an essay
- Create an outline

- Speak before a group of people
- Create a daily schedule
- How to handle failure

Business

- Keep a calendar
- Address an envelope
- Write a check
- Back up a computer
- Take care of belongings
- Organize passwords

Employment

- Write a resume
- Write a cover letter
- Write thank you notes
- How to find a job

Health and Safety

- Know medical history
- Understand basic nutrition
- Understand the need for sleep

- Understand basic fitness
- Make and keep medical appointments
- Situational awareness
- Emergency preparedness

Nearly Adult: Young Adults Launched and Learning

When setting your child off into the world, there are three keys to the transition.

1. Keep your five year plan in mind. In five years, you want to have a happy, healthy, and close extended family. When conflict occurs during college, keep this five year plan in mind.

2. Step in only when your child is being life-threateningly or life-alteringly stupid. They will make poor choices, but they can learn from them like you and I do every day. The only time you need to step in is when they are being

dangerously dumb. Believe me . . . it happens. Not often, but it happens.

3. Remember Scripture. One of the most common homeschooling Bible verses can still be your greatest encouragement. Proverbs 22:6 says "Train up a child in the way he should go, and when he is old he will not depart from it." Homeschool parents are responsible for the first portion of the verse. The Bible instructs us to "Train up a child in the way he should go." The Lord promises us a reward for our work, saying, "When he is old he will not depart from it." When you send your child into the world, you are in the middle section of this verse—the section that has only one thing to say, a comma. There is a long, dramatic pause between training them up and the promise at the end. That is your child's responsibility. Your part is letting go. You let go of your responsibility, and look with great anticipation to "when he is old."

I wish the promise was immediate and children who have been brought up in the "fear and admonition of the Lord" would never stray from the path. But you and I know this isn't true. Grown children make bad choices. Jesus hand-picked Judas as his disciple, and even being with Jesus daily for three years didn't prevent him from falling away. Sometimes teens make an absolutely confounding string of bad choices. At this point, however, you need to remember one important fact . . . your child is now an adult. Adults get to make their own bad choices, as we did so long ago.

Failure to Launch: Growing a Couch Potato

When children are unprepared for adulthood, and don't want to leave home, failure is a possibility. Often called "couch potatoes," some young people live at home, skating through life without responsibilities, lacking the tools to transition to adulthood. Instead, they choose the path of least resistance, floating down the river of life without making their own way, like a pinball bouncing around as their parents intervene. They may be coddled by parents who are trying to help, but are instead causing harm. If you miss the window of opportunity, the launch sequence can become thwarted. Like teaching your child to read when they are ready, you also need to launch them when they are ready. And like learning to read, eventually you'll need to provide detailed instruction if they don't begin to catch on.

To thrive, adults need to experience both independence and responsibility. When we remove these two keys, we are causing our children to grow into couch potatoes.

Adults: Healthy Boundaries with Grown Adult Children

Set clear expectations about how long your child may live at home. You might explain that they can receive support and live at home if they have a full-time job or attend college full time. Explain how long you will extend this offer, and when they will be expected to move out after they begin a career. With clear expectations that they will receive no spending money, phone privileges, or gas for the car, they may become more motivated to make a positive life choice. You may even want to charge rent after a certain point.

Often called "Velcro Parents" or "Helicopter Parents," well-meaning moms and dads can stand in the way of progress, preventing their children from growing up. Avoid enabling their bad behavior by allowing them to experience negative consequences for their choices. Resist being codependent or overly clingy. Your need to be needed can be an albatross around your child's neck, preventing them from achieving success.

If you find yourself in a complicated or devastating situation, or simply want to learn how to parent an adult child, these are some books I recommend:

Engaging Today's Prodigal: Clear Thinking, New Approaches, and Reasons for Hope by Carol Barnier

Parenting Your Adult Child: How You Can Help Them Achieve Their Full Potential by Chapman and Campbell

Setting Boundaries with Your Adult Children: Six Steps to Hope and Healing for Struggling Parents by Allison Bottke. This book is geared primarily toward parents dealing with delinquent behavior: drugs, alcohol, and felonious behaviors.

When Our Grown Kids Disappoint Us: Letting Go of Their Problems, Loving

Them Anyway, and Getting on with Our Lives by Jane Adams, who provides warmth, empathy, and perspective.

The Power of Praying for Your Adult Children by Stormie Omartian will provide motivation and encouragement to pray daily for your children.

Parenting Today's Teens with Mark Gregston of Heartlight Ministries is a website that provides training, podcasts, and resources for struggling families of teenagers.

Bad things can happen to good parents. If you need help dealing with complex issues from alcoholism, to cutting, to anorexia, reach out for professional help.

Empty Nest: Homeschool Parents Left Behind

When your child launches, there is something big happening back in their childhood home. Parents are left behind.

The nest is empty. The children are gone, and the adjustment has begun. But what about you? The homeschool parent still at home? Toward the end of homeschooling, you start to wonder about the next stage of life. What will you do when you aren't homeschooling?

I can suggest what not to do. I heard a woman at the store talking about how bored she was with her life. She had attended four Weight Watchers meetings during the week, not because she was overweight, but because she was bored! Although I'm a big fan of Weight Watchers, I wondered, "Is this all there is to life?" The empty nest is not an end. It's a change—a beginning.

There are certain key things you can do to make this a gentle transition.

1. Give Yourself Away

Help other people. Volunteer or work at an endeavor that allows you to help people. Homeschoolers are helpers by nature. How can you support other homeschoolers? What can you do to make it easier for the next mother who is stressed out about homeschooling? Give yourself away in new ways, too! I began volunteering regularly at our local clothing bank. It's a wonderful feeling to do something so concrete and physical that will help people and this is the reason The HomeScholar was born all those years ago. There is nothing that can take your mind away from your own problems more than helping people with even bigger troubles!

2. Get What You Wished For

When I was homeschooling, I had to say "No" to fun things. I had kids at home, had to get dinner on the table, and there were 13 soccer practices to attend each week! When the kids are gone, now is your time to say "Yes!" to the fun things you have put off! My husband and I started singing in our church choir.

Evening practices aren't a hassle at all when you don't have to find a babysitter!

3. Make a List

While you are homeschooling high school, list everything you wish you could do. Think back on the past few years. What would have been fun? Your turn is coming soon, so creating a bucket list makes sense. Make a list of activities or volunteer positions that sound like fun. List homeschool organizations you would like to help. If you had plenty of time, how would you like to serve your community and your church? After years of serving your family, soon it will be your time to serve others.

4. Exercise and Aesthetics

After graduation, you also have time to take care of yourself. Do you have a box of photos and no time for scrapbooking? Or clutter around the house, with no time to organize? Think of all the great crafts you'll have time for! And when you retire from homeschooling, you can take care of yourself and finally be able to exercise. Just think, you can take a walk and stop to smell the roses!

5. Avoid Heart Aching Loneliness

You hear about the empty nest feeling when your children go to college. It's true—and it's probably unavoidable. But you can lessen the affects by being active in your church and community. Give yourself away. Soon it will be your turn to volunteer, serve, and have fun! Your turn is coming, and you can make the best of it!

Homeschool Advantage: A Healing Balm Covering Regrets

All parents have deep emotions when sending kids to college, not only homeschoolers. When you feel a tug on your heart, it's not because you are a homeschool parent—it's because you are a parent. Your heart may hurt, but homeschooling can be a healing balm.

Homeschooling high school can minimize regrets once your children are grown. With the ability to shape and mold character while educating, your children will have the best possible chance of success. Letting go can come with no regrets!

I was surprised by an article in The New York Times, "Students, Welcome to College; Parents, Go Home."

As the latest wave of superinvolved parents delivers its children to college, institutions are building into the day, normally one of high emotion, activities meant to punctuate and speed the separation. It is part of an increasingly complex process, in the age of Skype and twice-daily texts home, in which colleges are urging "Velcro parents" to back off so students can develop independence.

Also according to the article:

> In order to separate doting parents from their freshman sons, Morehouse College in Atlanta has instituted a formal "Parting Ceremony."

Super-involved, Velcro parents? This does not describe me. I worked hard to teach my children independence. I remember taking my own children to college. As a parent, saying goodbye was emotional. But mostly, I felt proud.

When Kevin was married, I thought I would cry a lot. I came prepared with fancy hankies and packages of Kleenex, just to be safe. But, you know what? I wasn't sad! I was happy. All day long, even during the ceremony, I didn't cry at all. My husband didn't cry either (another surprise). Our overwhelming emotion was joy. After four years of dating and four years of college, we had already said our goodbyes, moved him away from home, and had complete confidence in his choice of a spouse. All that was left was happiness.

I did notice one thing, as I said my goodbyes at college. I had no regrets. I knew without a doubt they were academically prepared. I knew they were prepared for any assault on their worldview. I knew that I had shaped and molded their character and behaviors to the best of my ability. Their life was now up to them.

Final Note

I have heard from many parents recently, who have reinforced a recurring theme of mine—that homeschool parents need to prepare their homeschool transcripts and save them forever. Parents are being called on to produce high school transcripts for children who graduated 5, 10, or 20 years ago! This is because their children are delaying entrance into college, are going back to get advanced degrees, or are being asked to produce records when applying for a new job.

Since *forever* is such a long time, here are some ideas to keep you from being caught off guard.

6 Ways to Save Homeschool Records Forever

You don't have to save your curriculum forever, and you don't have to save all your child's daily work or notebooks or papers. But you do need to save the *official* homeschool records forever. In my class, "Homeschool Records That Open Doors," I will help you discover just what kind of homeschool records you need to make (and, of course, keep).

Forever is a long time. This is what I suggest:

1. Save your work on your computer in an easy-to-find folder, clearly labeled with a title and child's

name.

2. Save a physical copy by printing it out and storing it in a file. Many people also save a physical copy in their safe deposit box with other important records like your mortgage information and car title.

3. Save a digital copy in a portable drive or on a disk. Again, some people will store that in their safe deposit box.

4. Email yourself a copy, so you can keep that in your email folders should you ever need it. Again, it needs to be easy to find, so make sure it's clearly labeled with a title and the child's name.

5. Email a copy to your child or family member so someone else will have a copy. This provides a backup system. I suggest sending that in PDF format, so it can't be

altered.

6. Use an online backup system such as Carbonite so it is safe and secure but also easy to replace if you need it.

Appendix 1

The Senior Year Home Stretch

Are you approaching the senior year home stretch? The final year of high school includes one main task: complete those college applications. It's not quite as simple as it sounds—it's a time-consuming process. College applications take a lot of time to complete and every college has its own process, its own forms, and its own requirements.

The First Day

Start on the first day of senior year (or even earlier if possible)! Double check the admission deadlines for colleges you're interested in—some even encourage applications in July or August. Be sure to begin filling out those applications in the summer before senior year if your child is going to be taking dual enrollment classes at community college, as they may not have the time and energy to do so during the year. Some colleges award admission and scholarships on a first-come first-served basis, so being the early bird could pay off.

Application Essays

College applications often mean writing many self-reflective, technically perfect essays. It takes a lot of time to write, edit, get input from others, revise, and rewrite them. The prospect of writing something self-reflective can be difficult or even scary for teens. Ensure there is plenty of time set aside for pre-writing. Put your English curriculum aside for a while and begin writing college application essays on the first day of senior year. This could count as a unit study on essay writing!

Forms and Deadlines

College application forms can be complex with many strangely worded questions. They usually ask for letters of recommendation and it can be difficult to decide whom to ask to write them. Make sure you give the letter writers plenty of time to put together their letters, and allow time to let the letters arrive at the colleges. Stay organized and be prepared! Those deadlines are firm and inflexible. Spend time in advance on the whole application process. Keep everything organized on a calendar. Mark every detail and deadline on it. Start early so those deadlines don't sneak up on you.

Homeschool Transcripts

Make sure those transcripts and course descriptions are completed by fall of senior year! Colleges want high school transcripts submitted by their application deadlines. Make sure your transcript includes classes that will be taken during senior year. If calculus is planned, put calculus on the transcript. Just don't include a final grade for classes that are not completed yet—indicate that the grade is TBD (to be determined) or IP (in progress).

Course Descriptions

And the transcript isn't all you'll be asked for—make sure you write complete course descriptions for each class. When applying to selective colleges, when your child has a strong preference for a certain college, or if you are relying on scholarships, these course descriptions are particularly important. They can also strengthen any applications. A course description should include a paragraph on what you did, a list of what was used, and details on how you determined grades.

Complete Records

Colleges may also require other records. A reading list, including books read for school and pleasure, may be requested. Samples of work (even in the student's own handwriting), may be asked for, or an activity and awards list, or a resume. Don't be surprised if they request a statement from you, the homeschool parent. You may want to write a cover letter for the transcript as well. Colleges can ask for some strange things. Plan ahead so you have the time for all these incidentals.

Repeat Tests

There are other priorities along with completing college applications. If you need to write tests, be sure to register for the first testing opportunity of the year so you get test results early. If SAT or ACT tests were taken and the scores could be improved upon, have your child repeat the tests. If you find subject tests are required, schedule them as well.

Fill Gaps

If there are any gaps in your child's education, fill them now. It may be as simple as including a one-semester economics course in senior year. If it's a big gap, such as missing a whole high school career's worth of foreign language credits, your child may need to take it in community college, or at least explain it on the applications.

FAFSA Fun

The Free Application for Federal Student Aid (FAFSA) is available to be completed online on October 1st of senior year. The government uses the FAFSA to decide how much money they believe you can afford to pay for college. You'll have the distinct pleasure of filling it out every year, from senior year of high school through senior year of college. The sooner you fill out the

FAFSA the better, because they give out financial aid on a first-come first-served basis and you don't want to miss out!

Seek Scholarships

After college applications are submitted, there are three waves of scholarships. The first is based on SAT and ACT scores and the GPA. The second is based on the FAFSA. The third is based on other factors such as merit, and may not come in until May of senior year or later. Between March and June, parents are on tenterhooks as they know students are admitted to college, but have no idea if they can afford to pay for it. This can be a stressful time. Continue to keep in touch with admission representatives and try to be patient!

Expect Change

This may be shocking, but teenagers change their minds! One day they will declare they are going to go to college far away, and the next they will say they never want to leave home. Sometimes situations change as well. Be prepared and try to plan ahead. Your senior may resist all the tasks they need to complete during their final year. Seniors are often 18 years old. Adults don't do what their parents tell them to do sometimes, and sometimes seniors don't either! Be prepared for your teenager to make adult decisions. But realize that it's possible they may be paralyzed by fear. Get as many tasks done as possible a year ahead, to make this transition year go more smoothly.

Panic Plan

While the best success comes to families who begin the college application process early, "second best" is possible. If you have a senior and have been unaware of the college admission process, success is still possible. Don't panic! Drop everything and work on those college applications and everything mentioned above, *now*. Take my "Getting the Big Scholarships" and "Finding a College" online courses for help. When you've completed the whole process, you can return to your regularly scheduled homeschool program.

Enjoy Success

Enjoy homeschooling your child for their final year! It's a tremendously busy time, filled with wild emotional highs and lows for both the parent and the child. Next year, when they have moved on to the next stage, you will look back longingly on this time of chaos. Stop laughing, it's true! Just ask friends who've already been through it . . . they'll tell you.

Appendix 2

Stigma-Free Homeschool Graduation

Once upon a time, colleges sometimes required a GED from homeschoolers before providing financial aid. Since 1998, however, Congress has provided a better way for homeschoolers to demonstrate their "ability to benefit" from federal financial aid. The law states that students who have "completed a secondary school education in a home school setting that is treated as a home school or a private school under state law" can receive federal financial aid. When you fill out the FAFSA, the government will decide how much financial aid you should receive. Your child can receive financial aid as a homeschool student, and does *not* have to take a GED.

The U.S. Department of Education's regulations explain that a student is eligible for financial aid if he was homeschooled, and either (1) obtained a secondary school completion credential as provided by state law, or (2) has completed a secondary school education in a homeschool setting under state law. What does this mean? If you are homeschooling within your state homeschool law, then your student is eligible for federal financial aid. There is no need to take the GED.

GED Stigma

I saw a movie the other day about a high school dropout. She wanted to get a good job, but couldn't without a high school diploma. She studied hard, and finally got her GED, proving that she had a high school education. It was a heart-warming story, but it illustrates one thing; a GED can carry the stigma of "high school dropout." Many homeschoolers prefer to avoid this stigma. Homeschoolers are *not* high school drop-outs! Homeschoolers are recognized under the law, as shown above. Our homeschool transcript is a real transcript. Our homeschool diploma is official. Our students can receive federal financial aid, as private and public school students do. In the working world, when the application asks if your child is a high school graduate, the answer is "yes." If the application asks if your child has a high school diploma, the answer is "yes."

Calculate your EFC

How much money are we talking about? How much federal financial aid is at stake? You may want to use one of the free online calculators to determine your estimated financial aid. When you estimate financial aid with the Expected Family Contribution calculator, remember it does *not* include merit scholarships. There is a good FAFSA calculator on the FAFSA website, fafsa.ed.gov.

A GED Requirement is *not* Homeschool Friendly

When you begin to contact colleges, ask them about their policy regarding homeschool students. They do not need a GED from your student. If they require a GED, you can bet they are not a homeschool friendly college. Some colleges allow a GED from homeschool students who do not provide either a transcript or portfolio. This is an option colleges use to provide flexibility in their homeschool admission policy. However, allowing a GED as an option is different than requiring a GED as part of their policy.

Get to know the college admission policy to determine if the school is homeschool friendly. Few colleges these days require a GED. Most colleges see and admit homeschoolers regularly, and are unfazed by homeschool transcripts. If you run across one that doesn't understand homeschooling, you should likely shop for another college—one that is more homeschool friendly. Colleges are increasingly learning that these sorts of policies are counter-productive and are changing them to be more accepting of homeschoolers. As homeschoolers in college become more common, colleges will feel growing pressure to take down barriers that discourage homeschool families. This is good news for families considering homeschooling high school.

Afterword

Who is Lee Binz and What Can She Do for Me?

Number one best-selling homeschool author, Lee Binz is The HomeScholar. Her mission is "helping parents homeschool high school." Lee and her husband, Matt, homeschooled their two boys, Kevin and Alex, from elementary through high school.

Upon graduation, both boys received four-year, full tuition scholarships from their first choice university. This enables Lee to pursue her dream job—helping parents homeschool their children through high school.

On The HomeScholar website, you will find great products for creating homeschool transcripts and comprehensive records to help you amaze and impress colleges.

Find out why Andrew Pudewa, Founder of the Institute for Excellence in Writing says, "Lee Binz knows how to navigate this often confusing and frustrating labyrinth better than anyone."

You can find Lee online at:

HomeHighSchoolHelp.com

If this book has been helpful, could you please take a minute to write us a quick review on Amazon? Thank you!

Testimonials

Such Wise Counsel

Lee, you are a wealth of knowledge! I just love this Gold Care Club! I'm making adjustments to the transcript, and I have a couple more questions for next week's phone consultation. Thanks for all the web links and CLEP testing information. I think you're an incredible woman, and I feel so blessed that God has provided me with such wise counsel.

~ Sherry in Washington

What a Relief!

I joined the Gold Care Club the same week our fourth child was born. Since then, I've spent many late night feedings on The HomeScholar website getting ready for middle school with our oldest child and watching How-to Training Courses. I feel a great sense of peace and excitement about homeschooling middle school.

What a relief to have an expert I can come to with my questions. I have so enjoyed my Gold Care Club Membership!! I tell my homeschool friends all about it. I'm excited to start practicing and using the things you've taught me as we begin middle school.

Thanks for all your help!

~ René and Baby

For more information about my **Comprehensive Record Solution** and **Gold Care Club**, go to:

www.ComprehensiveRecordSolution.com
www.GoldCareClub.com

Lee Binz, The HomeScholar

Also From The HomeScholar...

- The HomeScholar Guide to College Admission and Scholarships: Homeschool Secrets to Getting Ready, Getting In and Getting Paid (Book and Kindle Book)

- Setting the Records Straight—How to Craft Homeschool Transcripts and Course Descriptions for College Admission and Scholarships (Book and Kindle Book)

- TechnoLogic: How to Set Logical Technology Boundaries and Stop the Zombie Apocalypse

- Finding the Faith to Homeschool High School

- The Easy Truth About Homeschool Transcripts (Kindle Book)

- Parent Training A la Carte (Online Training)

- Total Transcript Solution (Online Training, Tools and Templates)

- Comprehensive Record Solution (Online Training, Tools and Templates)

- High School Solution (Online Training, Tools, Resources, and Support)

- College Launch Solution (Online Training, Tools, Resources, and Support)

- Gold Care Club (Comprehensive Online Support and Training)

- Silver Training Club (Online Training)

The HomeScholar Coffee Break Books Released or Coming Soon on Kindle and Paperback:

- Delight Directed Learning: Guiding Your Homeschooler Toward Passionate Learning

- Creating Transcripts for Your Unique Child: Help Your Homeschool Graduate Stand Out from the Crowd

- Beyond Academics: Preparation for College and for Life

- Planning High School Courses: Charting the Course Toward High School Graduation

- Graduate Your Homeschooler in Style: Make Your Homeschool Graduation Memorable

- Keys to High School Success: Get Your Homeschool High School

Started Right!

- Getting the Most Out of Your Homeschool This Summer: Learning just for the Fun of it!

- Finding a College: A Homeschooler's Guide to Finding a Perfect Fit

- College Scholarships for High School Credit: Learn and Earn With This Two-for-One Strategy!

- College Admission Policies Demystified: Understanding Homeschool Requirements for Getting In

- A Higher Calling: Homeschooling High School for Harried Husbands (by Matt Binz, Mr. HomeScholar)

- Gifted Education Strategies for Every Child: Homeschool Secrets for Success

- College Application Essays: A Primer for Parents

- Creating Homeschool Balance: Find Harmony Between Type A and Type Zzz...

- Homeschooling the Holidays: Sanity Saving Strategies and Gift Giving Ideas

- Your Goals this Year: A Year by Year Guide to Homeschooling High School

- Making the Grades: A Grouch-Free Guide to Homeschool Grading

- High School Testing: Knowledge That Saves Money

- Getting the BIG Scholarships: Learn Expert Secrets for Winning College Cash!

- Easy English for Simple Homeschooling: How to Teach, Assess and Document High School English

- Scheduling—The Secret to Homeschool Sanity: Plan You Way

Back to Mental Health

- Junior Year is the Key to High School Success: How to Unlock the Gate to Graduation and Beyond

- Upper Echelon Education: How to Gain Admission to Elite Universities

- How to Homeschool College: Save Time, Reduce Stress and Eliminate Debt

- Homeschool Curriculum That's Effective and Fun: Avoid the Crummy Curriculum Hall of Shame!

- Comprehensive Homeschool Records: Put Your Best Foot Forward to Win College Admission and Scholarships

- Options After High School: Steps to Success for College or Career

- How to Homeschool 9th and 10th Grade: Simple Steps for Starting Strong!

- Senior Year Step-by-Step: Simple Instructions for Busy Homeschool Parents

- How-to-Homeschool Independently: Do-it-Yourself Secrets to Rekindle the Love of Learning

- High School Math The Easy Way: Simple Strategies for Homeschool Parents in Over Their Heads

- Homeschooling Middle School with Powerful Purpose: How to Successfully Navigate 6th through 8th Grade

- Simple Science for Homeschooling High School: Because Teaching Science isn't Rocket Science!

Would you like to be notified when we offer the next Coffee Break Books for FREE during our Kindle promotion days? If so, leave your name and email below and we will send you a reminder.

HomeHighSchoolHelp.com/
freekindlebook

Visit my Amazon Author Page!

amazon.com/author/leebinz

Made in the USA
Columbia, SC
24 January 2022

54109583R00059